Language is a Queer Thing

An India:UK Writing Exchange

PUBLISHED BY VERVE POETRY PRESS
https://vervepoetrypress.com
mail@vervepoetrypress.com

FIRST PUBLISHED SEP 2022

Printed and bound in the UK
by Imprint Digital, Exeter

ISBN: 978-1-913917-24-1

CONTENTS

About the poets and organisers

INTRODUCTION by The VERVE Team

Language is a Queer Thing is a project which pairs three India based queer poets with three UK based queer poets in an online exchange followed by two residencies - one in Birmigham leading into BBC Contains Strong Language Festival 2022, and one in Mumbai leading into Tata Literature Live! The project has been created and organised by VERVE Poetry Festival, Birmingham, and The Queer Muslim Project, Delhi and funded by British Council, India as part of its India:UK Cultural Echange Season.

As part of the online section of the exchange, and in response to online workshops and discussion forums, we asked our poets to produce poems alongside their partners to appear in this anthology and which will be performed to an audience, but also to each other, at the two festivals, one in the UK and one in India.

We have been thrilled with the results, as our poets have engaged with the subject of their own and each others' queer experience, and worked to find ways of communicating with us and each other by queering the English language where possible. From joy to fear, from feeling misunderstood to feeling whole, the queer experience is portrayed and communicated in ways as varied as the poems that contain it.

We hope you learn something and feel something from engaging with these wonderful new works, as we have.

Aug 2022.

Language is a Queer Thing

Hatchlings
Megha Harish

For 110 million years turtles have been using the earth's magnetic field to find their way back to their birthplace.

I don't know why they don't teach us these things to convince us that middle-school physics is applicable in the real world. I'd pick turtles over iron filings every day of the week.

When the nesting season arrives, female loggerheads will return to the beaches where they were born to lay their eggs.

Who said women don't make good navigators? Imagine being able to make your way back to a memory after decades. Nostalgia lives in our blood – warm and cold.

Female turtles do not possess the mammalian maternal instinct. They leave their nests and subsequent hatchlings to fend for themselves.

I wonder if it is admirable to be toughened by abandonment.

The sex of baby turtles is determined by the temperature of the sand (+/- 29 degrees celsius)

Who gets to tell us who we are?

Loggerhead eggs hatch after 50 to 60 days. Hatchlings wait underneath the surface until sunset to emerge from their nests and make their way towards the ocean.

Waiting for the safest time and conditions gives us the best shot.

Only 1 in 1000 turtles survives to maturity.

When singing the praises of the one who breaks glass ceilings, whisper a word of remembrance for the ones who made thousands of cracks before, but didn't survive the blow.

The first part of migration is called the 'frenzy period' which involves almost continuous swimming for 24-36 hours.

But struggle is rewarded with freedom.

As juveniles, Cabo Verdean loggerheads migrate up to 12,000km across the Atlantic.

In leaving, we find home within ourselves.

For the next 15 years they will drift around during what is known as "The Lost Years."

I don't know what they're getting up to. But I know they're not lost.

Subterranea
Megha Harish

The agnostic in me went diving. Along with the anxious one. They had a panic attack in the water. This hadn't happened since that one a few years ago on the intercity train. Both and neither wanted to turn back, ascend. Their thumbs go up – the only way to speak. Let's go. Inhale. Exhale. Repeat. Let's stay. The ocean rewards perseverance. They let me carry on. 30 minutes later, in my first ever underwatercurrent, the anxious one is jolted back into action

am I imagining this
or am I moving?

It's okay. The others are swaying too, their breath now escaping in bubble helixes. Some other others join the sway. Loggerhead turtles. Snacking on seagrass. Swimming. Meditating. Floating around in the blue light, at home in the ebb and flow. Like pendulum phone flashlights to a ballad at a concert we can't hear. The ocean rewards. Even the agnostic one sees angel wings in the flippers.

The next day we're 29 metres down, in a volcanic cave on the island's underbelly. Torches land on fallen shark denticles in a seabed of discarded / left behind / remains. Above land, I struggle to find the words with which to explain. In the van we all speak different languages, coming together over some shared English and rudimentary Portuguese, grateful for shared etymologies. How to convey that sea urchin skeletons look just like their bodies in inverted colours – still spiky, all bone.

> We are dust
> and to dust we return.

Milk bikis
Megha Harish

Like Roger, if I speak
of paradise, then I'm speaking
of my grandmother. Who taught
me that the biggest joy
lies in the little joys.

One pandemic online grocery shop,
I ordered the biscuits of my childhood summers.
"Kannu mooku" biscuits
we used to call them, white vanilla
cream smiling through the face-shaped cut outs.
I tasted them. They weren't the same anymore.

Stocking the kitchen
with your favourite snacks
before each visit, I realised I'd learnt to love
from her too. She wouldn't
have wanted me to conceal
myself or my becoming. Britannia
is the name of an Indian company, if you
can believe it (est. 1892). They make
two variants. I buy the plain ones now.

Paradise
Amani Saeed & Megha Harish

Poets don't often collaborate. They also don't usually explain a poem or how it came together – death of the author and all. But we did collaborate, and we wanted to tell you that it happened over the phone, after a conversation about love and form and grandmothers, and that through some alchemy, or perhaps just mutual understanding, our late night freewrites turned into morning revelations. Sometimes, it's important to understand not just where we arrive, but how we get there.

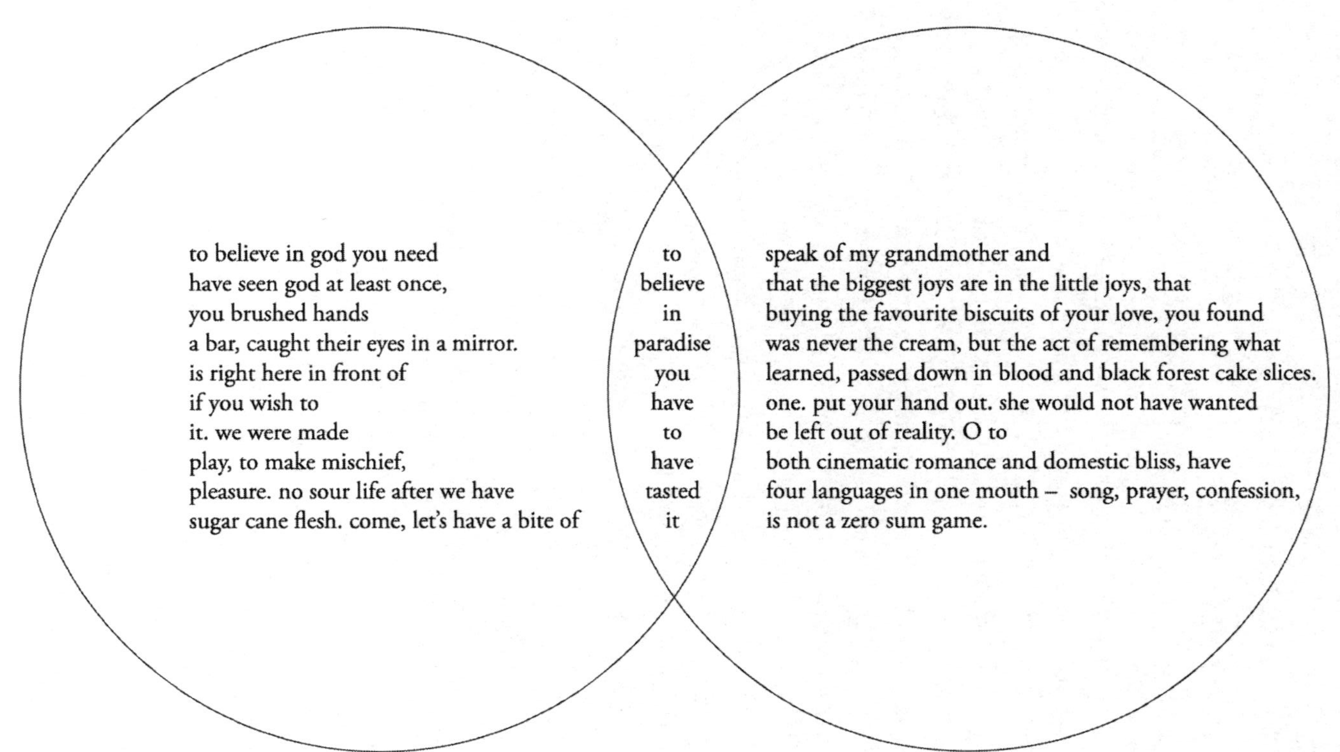

13

Ganna
Amani Saeed

To believe in paradise you need to have tasted paradise. To believe in god you need to have seen god at least once, brushed hands in a lift, locked eyes across the bar. To see you need to look. To look you need to raise your head up. Raise your head up. Put your hand out. Good things are in front of you if you wish to take them. A friend said hell is a place god is not. For us there is no hell, only the number of footsteps between each other. My love, we were not made for a sour life. We were made for sugar cane flesh, for play, for mischief, for pleasure. Come, and let me praise you from head to toe. Come, and let me curl my hand under your chin and lift your gaze up. Look up.

Tell me what you see.

Omen
Amani Saeed

I just want to live a beautiful life. Expand beyond this bedroom corner of the universe. I want to be to god what waves are to the ocean. I want to trust that these feet, once lifted from the sea floor, will propel us forward. Come,

let me measure your lips with mine, four across, two high. Open your mouth, let me place a piece of halwa inside. It's not so hard, is it, to split a cardamom pod and spill the seeds into your hand. To cut through the air like a stream of mint tea into a waiting glass.

I want to drench my tongue in vermouth and kiss you. Negronis on the counter behind us, spliff in hand. Brisk Sunday breeze. Sade wafting through the air. I want to become dear to you, let you become dear to me. To have joy

is to have absolute conviction. To advance through the city, the burning forest, the clearing, to the single point in the horizon only you and god can see.

Somewhere there is a sky for us. There is a world that you and I are allowed to simply enjoy. In this world, we'll know how to love and be loved, how to surrender and be surrendered to. One night, I swear, I'll come home with nothing but good things to tell you.

Riis beach
Amani Saeed

I'd never seen water so damn gay.
Never seen so many breasts out, never tasted
ocean so salty, so playful, never been claimed

as someone's child before. When we entered the water,
she gave me a seashell to shove down my swimsuit.
I thought she wanted me to keep it safe.

Instead it cupped me like armour, as if it knew
that to protect was to comfort.
Then she indulged us with waves. Tossed them

like frisbees, some low– which we giggled over –
some high– that we flung ourselves under– and some
we didn't see coming. Those ones earned us

back-of-the-head-slaps, but she was only being
a good teacher. We knew she was preparing us,
that she only wanted us to pay attention, to listen

for the underbelly. To know when to jump, when
to plunge, how to find the sweet spot where bodies
become foam and our laughter

answers questions I didn't know I asked.

kanpur is shrinking in the rearview mirror
Sanah Ahsan

after Agha Shahid Ali

i want to hold origin in my mouth -

      the 1857 uprising   bethel leaf and katha paste

bassy adhaan   ripening rekhti   big tofu tits   we

lick the back of the queen's face until
it envelops me an Individual I am
folded wet to empire fuck dainty ears
thin-lipped blonde blue bluer i become bendable
light escaping the start of my skin
whimpering urdu watches from the closet
colourless rain makes a splash on soil
that never asked to be watered down

two million corpses pave the road to pakistan
and kanpur is shrinking in the rearview mirror
the midwife wraps soft cloth around
tightly-wound curls my mother's thumb
learning baby bone she whispers
into the tiny land of my ear *i can't*
i can't i'm not sure why i can't

cord
Sanah Ahsan

I'm ashamed of ~~giving~~ birth to you
I'm not
I'm ~~ashamed of giving~~ birth to you
I'm ashamed of giving birth to you

She says it in white font against a blue bubble.
A framed picture I can't unsee. I can just about type: *I know this is hurting you.* To think of all the phones my mother has ever held. The cream corded landline plugged into the raised walnut walls of her bedroom: her immaculately manicured finger pressing its circular buttons with large-print numbers. Dialling possibility. A father once wrapped its cord around her neck like a scarf. Flesh folding under each coil - the lines bending, even then. It took tiny fingers to free her.

shezada
Sanah Ahsan

       i have my father's little toe
stubborn little shit that refuses to touch

       the floor in spring he wears woollen indoors
heat rolled up halfway makes a qubba on his silver head

       he eats kichdi with his good hand
teeth stained by paan, amber leaf, exhibits of indiscipline

       i know six am by his humming
aweless lungs make sounds for help

       he asks me to write a letter to his boss
what could i teach a failing memory

       he is a sha'ir in urdu bangla punjabi but labours
over rungs painted milk white   when he doesn't know

       the answer to my climbing
questions his smile says *ask the google* my father is still

       that little boy who pissed on a Karachi djinn tree
swears it had him English   speaking fluent out of nowhere

       he places bets on miracles   in Shangri-
London he buys a lottery-ticket everyday   my date of birth his

talisman i win him disapproval he keeps playing
the same numbers trusting he made me   a bed everyday undoes

        its making he ruins me Shero-Shayaris splinters them halfenglish
and when my girlfriend maalishes his feet playing the dream

        daughter i could never be   he rises into sleep
little toe flying free   from the edge of a strewn blanket

Looking for Shrapnels
Garfield F. Dsouza

"Why are you leaving me?"
was my colour that day,
swathed in the knives
of a conversation
constructed in the confines of a bus.

"Why won't you touch me?"
perfumed out of my fingertips
that suffocated in my fists.
It wore the armour
of a bite into the flesh I never bit into.

"Was it the sex we never had?"
groped my groins firmly into my trousers.
I didn't quite like its touch: it was naked
and didn't have the decency
of lying in a mess that wasn't my own.

"Are you bored of me?"
I carried in my pocket:
It's a favourite. I tap its melody
out of my shirt every time
I need to find the mops
for the bathroom.
This time though,
I wanted to hear
something else.

"Did you—ever—love me at all?"
lay choked
under the sugar in the latte.
Bitter almonds
was not particularly its flavour.

I was by the seaside,
walking
with a pair of puppy-dog eyes
that had swallowed
my voice of reason.

I was looking for answers, you know:
those shrapnels
that wear icicles and strangle
ears neatly into ashen haemoglobin
charred to the left in your ribs.

What I found
was the moan of time
(or the lack of it)
recited by the dog
And some excuses
curtained by the spit
of silence
deaf enough to flood my mouth.

I don't quite remember what happened next.

I think I was on the bus.
No wait, I took a train back—I think.
I was naked,
pulling my skin close for comfort;
I was rummaging through photographs
in the folds of my plasma—
just as they jumped
into the buffet of amnesia
being served
on the blurring rails
I bent down to pacify.

I have no idea on what stove
my blood froze either,
what strand of hair
boiled to an acrid brown in the freezer—

I don't remember, really.

I only remember writing this
several years later
on the footboard of a carriage;
A carriage that tiptoed
across the creek
at 11 in the night,
all the while hoping its passenger
would hold its arm,
step back,
and choose to drown
in the city lights
on the other side of the creek.

2012
Garfield F. Dsouza

It was the year I said to myself
I'll take a job in a remote city
and start life anew.

By that, I didn't mean I'd live in a thatched hut,
draw water from the well,
and coax the cows to moo.

I wanted what you'd know
as erasure:
A complete evaporation of all memory
Of all the he-hens I danced with,
Of all the asses I'd travelled on,
And, of course, of all the ones
Who owned all of those.

You see, I had it all figured out.
Erasure to me was supremely simple—
Almost like following
the numerous steps
and the rinse-and-repeats
of an ordinary recipe.

All you have to do is:
First, call Father and ask him to send you some bread.
      Then, say hello to a body
      by the name of Mary—
      Do it the old-fashioned way:

"Hail Mary!" it seems is how it's done.
Tell her she's graceful and all that,
and repeat that around ten times or so.
Then go back to calling on Father:
This time, tell him what a great guy he is
and that you're scared of him and all that.
And then, after that, help yourself to some divine spirit.

AND then repeat ALL of that
with a believable pretence of sincerity
five times once a day.

If that's not getting you anywhere,
Spruce up the proceedings
with a litany of lamentation.

Lament about every lap you danced into.
Rue the balls you threw.
And woe betide the ass you rode.

Lament long enough
and loud enough
for your neighbours
to forget the telly
and tune in to you.

Lament as if your life depends on it
Yell: "Why me? Why me Lord?
What have I ever done?"
Even if what you've done
seems right to you.

Remember to stir it all
at the appropriate decibel.
The louder,
The better the chances
that what you've done
will start to seem wrong.

And then, every Friday,
Mix it all in a frying pan,
blest with some olive oil;
Light a consecrated fire
and scream it all
to a blood-curdling boil.

And voila! All the ingredients
will leap into the air
as if you've whipped their bottoms
And disappear!
And an electronic voice
fed on a diet of zeroes and ones
will exclaim: "E-ray-sheer kompleat."

Well, needless to say,
I'm happy to report
the recipe was a runaway success:
In the end, something did disappear.
For after all those blasted years,
I'm here,
I'm queer,
And well, I've gotten used to it.

Spaces
Garfield F. Dsouza

Well, I don't think I have much of an opinion about them.
Youknowthethingaboutthemis
they   somehow   seem   rather
odd   awkward, actually
YouseewhatImsaying?

It's as if a toddler
has scribbled
all   over   the   page
and the mother
is finding it hard
to keep up with all the washing up
she has to do
in its wake.

Oh wait! That was a bad analogy.

No! Wait! It works!

See, the toddler
is me
scribbling the place with white
spaces
And you are the mother/father whatever
inspecting each space
and wondering
and grasping
at the sense I'm trying to make.

Makes sense now?

Well, I've been told
it's absolutely fabulous
in its affair with
silence.

Both make love to each other
as if there were no tomorrow.
If a   is here,
silence is
next to it,
above it,
below it,
in it!—
There's no stopping those two!

Not to mention the times it fills in for when you have so much to say
that you'd rather say
nothing at all.
And of course for the times when you really do want to say
nothing at all.

Speaking of spaces, did I tell you
apartments in Mumbai can hardly
be considered spacious at all?
I m e a n s e v e n o f t h e m
w o u l d e a s i l y f i t i n t o a l l t h e
s p a c e I h a v e u s e d h e r e .

Just like my life at one point in time.
It all fit into a tiny little week over and over again...

I would usually meet someone on Sunday.
Flirt till Tuesday.
Fall in love on Wednesday.
Plan a date on Thursday.
Arrive on a date on Saturday.
And then go back to hunt on Sunday.

I don't know about my dates,
but I for one,
made it a point to inspect
the space between their legs.
With that information in hand,
I would look up at
the space between their lips.
I never took into consideration
the space between their ears.
Probably, because I myself had none
or mine wasn't working at all!

But somewhere d
       o
       w
        n the line, all that changed.
Probably because the space between my legs
decided to sell itself—
well, most of itself—
to the one between my ears.

So I don't think I need to bother really.
In fact, I didn't even need to
go through all the trouble of writing all of this
just to convince myself to
Go ahead

Take a chance
And use that biiiig white space.

Because
if there's no room for change
And no room for improvement
Between what I call my ears
Then there'll be no room
for some of this   as well.

                e
l   m
     o
h   v
                e

anil pradhan

love gave me a new yew twig to put inside my wallet
and before i could ask, he said: this will keep you safe
as you prepare to leave ~~my~~ this home in the northills
that would be yours if you ~~could~~ change your mind
but home is never (t)here, it doesn't wait in courtyards
but, i remind myself of seeking solace in poison needles
sharp enough to ~~prick~~ pierce bleed my kintsugi heart out

≈ माया जस्तो घर जस्तो माया जस्तो घर जस्तो माया ≈

love gave me a cypress twig, put it in my right hand
& before i could sigh, he said: it will smell like ~~home~~ me
and make memory as you slither down the northills
that could've been yours if you'd arrived a bit earlier
but love is never moored, it fleets the eaves of time
so, i remind myself of smelling home in d(r)ying leaves
brittle enough to wilt into my ~~sore~~ palms, turn into blood

≈ माया जस्तो घर जस्तो माया जस्तो घर जस्तो माया ≈

love gave me a ripe passion fruit, burst it near my face
and before i could cry, he said: it'll be a bit bittersweet
for the grief of summer has seeped into these northills
now it is in your veins, like the dreams in your eyelids
but likeness is never an excuse, it is merely a consolation
i remind myself how it tricks the flux out of our minds
tired enough to let us mistake familiarity for namesakes

≈   माया जस्तो घर जस्तो माया जस्तो घर जस्तो माया   ≈

i gave love a home in the corners of my blue bedroom
and after i counted the verses, it said: write some more
trust the safe-keeping, the leave-taking, the namesaking
that linger at the far edges of your (p)arched human lips
but remember the mantra: love is like home is like love
they criss-cross the emptiness left by time's (tres)passing
echoing a sleep before having to find a reason to get lost

s
poetry
x
anil pradhan

i've come to think of sex as dangerous art
the way i have toiled for hours at the desk
at nights, after long days of laden sighs
i have created (im)mortal art in bed too
through the pen(i)s of lovers and beloveds
sustaining the flames of our imagination
manoeuvring our hands with/in passion
till warm poetry erupts in alabaster white
every moan a verse, every orgasm a poem
evoked from trembling lips: mine to his
echoed in nicotined mouths: his to mine
sharing our hea(r)t ~ tongue to tongue
painting our faces, feeding our hunger
with nectar as ephemeral as our dreams
such that love isn't l(u/o)st in translation
at times, i wish beloveds were lovers too
oh, oh, what poetry we would have made

brick-by-brick
anil pradhan

the old *kāli mandir* at *behālā thānā more* is gone
brick-by-brick, eroding slow in the makers' dereliction

at seven, i would climb up, become the goddess, and
through its terrifying bareness, in childhood grace
preside over the absence of murmurs afore the altar
as red as the ribs jutting out of puny human faith
reclaimed only by ambitious shrubs, hungry rats

at eleven, i could not visit the temple anymore, so
home became a construct, a receding dream, like
many milk teeth left as offerings to the gaping hole
lost footsteps no longer echo through the by-lanes
stinking of human piss, incense sticks, brass bells

at twenty-seven, what must i write for you today
so many years have been brushed under mortar
you must have your own temple at some corner
whose solace you can't embrace in late summer
so blunt, so sparse, human keepsakes for full moons
our own fading away then becomes a cautionary tale

there is a govt. school there, now, and god is dead
brick-by-brick, a new story upon a terribly old one

namesakes: two poems on love
anil pradhan & Ifẹ Grillo

act i - *anil*

matinā ~ the word lost its way three generations ago when grandma crossed a border and two holy rivers to arrive at the land of fishes that had strange names and left home, again, on a four decade old winter dawn without putting into my palms the three-syllabled word that would haunt me, like a half-seen dream, all the way from my mother's southern city to my father's northern hills where, in the quiet orchards, the plums are speckled in blood whispering to me, without haste, like a *lok dohori* repeating that i cannot carry this hunger away, in my empty hands and so the thrushes took pity & conjured for me a metonymy

māyā ~ the word that must suffice, upon our leave-taking after sojourning to a home that we can never say we had like a whiff of the rosemary that a lover rubbed on my lips as consolation, fermenting into sighs, turning into a fable eluding into the soft echo of the first of the human vowels of the oldest language we know: our fingers on human skin of oranges in winter, of clovers in june, of a sudden caress like a whisper dissolving into the goosebumps of his nape traversing his spine, toiling upon his loins, tickling his feet the way the *rangeet* flows into the *rangpo* into the *teestā* reminding ourselves of the need to touch ~ touch ~ touch

ifẹ ~ the word that is you is also a prayer across the seas
i often wonder why certain names reach us so late in life
some nights simply won't coagulate into a will-o'-the-wisp
sometimes, language can be quiet, a queer thing, like you
mean to say something else & end up saying exactly that
like people would end up calling you by your name and
still not know how to love you through the veil of silence
so we remind them how we named ancient cities after you
not knowing how desires get mistaken for something else
it's not an if, it's a how, it will linger as long as we breathe
and see our palms become palimpsests of loom(ing) memory

love ~ as they say, will make us do the queerest of things
like finding namesakes in the backyards of our own homes
only to realise: we need to leave if we want to arrive, so
one day, i will cross that single border and the two rivers
and clasp the word in the forgotten land, bring it for you
one day, i will swim up those three northern rivers too
and place the word into your palms, saying, take it, now
with *matinā* becoming *māyā* becoming love becoming us
one day, you will do it too, *ifẹ*: find home in your tongue
one day, you will too find a home for your name, because
you now know the bygone secret: to name is to never forget

act ii - *Ifẹ*

As I stand there, with your words
in my hands and your eyes on my frown,
I want to believe you.

I hold the phrases you whisper
like a delicate plate
that's only meant to be used when
guests come round.
I make a song out of the
reassurances you try to give me.

But I can't help asking myself
Why does your love feel like a magic trick?

I've seen your type before.
Alchemists who make a patchwork
out of stolen words
and morph it into a
Painting.
Who turn vowels into
bullets dressed up as moonlight picnics.
Who pick through the valley of languages to
carve out new meanings.

When you speak to me about love,
Why does it feel like I'm entering
a home I've never visited
but has my name
on the door?

Why does your love feel like a memory?
A travelled path along a road my
body wanted to go down?
A history book that has pages stuck together.
A whiff of rosemary that lingers
from a trip I was never on.

Because when I asked God for love,
I was given Wahala.
Told that love requires having a
home in yourself
so where would I
even put
it?

So when you say that love is my namesake
I put a hand on your cheek and
tell you that
I'm not sure that love goes here.

But then you look at me
make stillness out of my body
And force me to listen.
You hold me until
our breaths sync up.

And we stand there,
willing love to dance with the air,
make a noise
and show us its colour.

And when it finally does,
It's quiet but somehow manages
to fill the room and make it sparkle.

Because this love,
this love we share
this queer thing
this omnipresent whisper
was so silent in pronunciation,
that I never realised that
It always existed.

Lágbájá
Ifẹ Grillo

An Ode to Lágbájá

Growing up,
one of my favourite artists was Lágbájá.
With an Iya-Ilu in his hands,
and magic in his pen,
he became a leader in Nigeria's music scene.

His name was no name
Chosen to represent the common man and
Picked to give a platform to the quiet.
And while that was noble,
It should be known that there
was nothing common about Lágbájá.

Lágbájá was a mystery man.
Clothed in fine garments that
was made in a baptism of enigma.
He dressed like the world's most loud spy.

Lágbájá was a superhero.
He wore a face mask to conceal
his identity so you never saw him whole.
And while you couldn't see his face,
his eyes still had a wink to them.
They danced with you like
he knew a secret.

And when played saxophone,
It was like he was telling you,
in a secret language,
how the world really worked.

Because Lágbájá was always
trying to tell you something.
In between the skentele skontolo dances
And the love-filled chaos,
Was a radical man with a plan for his country.

Because Lágbájá knew that
we were nothing without community.
That art was nothing more than a mission statement.
That the revolution needed bass in its voice and
harmonies on its throat.
So he weaved politics into his music like a seamstress.
Made a John-Doe out of his name,
and got to work.

So when people ask me,
How it feels to feels
To wear green, white, and green,
but have a rainbow stripe running through me?

I tell them that Lágbájá
was the first time I understood
what it meant to be high camp.
That Lágbájá taught me that leaning into
the strange only makes us stronger.

That he showed me that sometimes we hide
ourselves,
not out of fear,
but out of purpose.

So when I chose to learn the sax
I knew it was because of him.
But it's only now I realise that he shows up
in the parts of me that have always
been made to feel like questions.
That he shows up in the parts of me
that want to set the room on fire.
That Lágbájá,
The nation's mystery man,
Was giving me clues all along.

I guess a man with
no name
no face
but a lot of heart,
and a love-filled message,
Gets to live forever

The are no mangoes in this poem
Ifẹ Grillo

The are no mangoes in this poem.
No mentions of honey being eaten while I
ponder my place,
and no bouquets of akara
being thrown at my feet.

I'm sorry to disappoint you but there are no
cultural metaphors in this poem.
So if I mention washing rice,
It is not an allegory for washing
away the pain of living as a minority,
It is because I wanted rice
the day I wrote this.

You may want to get out now because
there are no spices in this poem.
No mentions of an orange sky and
I have not compared a kiss to some
vaguely ethnic pleasant aroma.

And you may have loved the movie,
but Wakanda doesn't exist in this poem.
Which is to say that I'm not here
to sell you a picture
that you think you
already own.

If you ask me to write a poem about
the motherland,
I'll tell you that I've already tried.
Tried craft a story that didn't
feel an ancient proverb.
Thought about how to make a moment
out of memories I don't fully trust.

If you want me to write about
the motherland,
I'll first have to decide whether
I'm its child.
Whether any story I tell would
be even my own.
Whether I believe that I can love
someone I never get to see.

And if I'm being honest,
I'm scared that if I add my voice
It'll be an eraser to someone else's.
Because what if imperialism is contagious
and I'm starting to catch a cold?

So there are no saviours in this poem.
There's just people trying to
connect with a place they are scared
to admit they don't really know.
There's just people trying to find a way
to stake their claim but not
become a parasite.
There's just folks trying

hold on to something
because nothing feels like
theirs.

But I don't want to make a high life out
of a land that I don't have to
face the burdens of.
Because to love a place
is to have solidarity with its people

So there are no mangoes in this poem.
There's no rice,
Casava,
Èfọ́ riro,
or Yam.

There is just a boy
That's trying to listen
And trying to connect.

Polyglot Lover
Ifẹ Grillo

They say that people have different love languages.
That who we are as lovers is unique and complex.
And its not that I don't agree,
It's that I don't care.

Because when it comes to you:

If you say that you love in acts of service,
Then I will bring the wind to you
so you have a soft breeze to flirt with
your hair when you walk.
I will make Icarus out of my body and bring
you the sun if you're cold.
And I will build you flat-pack furniture
like it's the Sistine Chapel.

If you say that you love in words of affirmation,
then I will write you odes that sound like
gospel music.
I will invent words that have
never touched anyone's tongue.
And I will make resurrect dead languages
just to find a phrase that properly represents
who you are.

If you say that you love in gifts,
then I will buy you your favourite pastry
every Thursday morning.
I will find the three wise men and
get them to sell me their gold,
frankincense and myrrh.
And I will replace the AirPods you always
lose.

If you say that you love in quality time,
then I will take you to a garden of Eden
and lay with you till the moon
kicks the sun out of the sky.
I will freeze-time,
stop the earth from spinning and
stay in a moment with you.
And I will shatter every clock in the
world and recycle the glass to make
you a coffee table.

If you say that you love in physical touch,
then will massage your shoulders,
run my hands through your hair
and draw out the tension from your body
like a magnet.
I will hold you like we're the only
two people left on earth and
the space between us is threatening our survival.
And I will attach my skin to yours,
make your body levitate
and sent it into orbit.

You could tell me that you love me
in a thousand languages,
and I would understand each one perfectly
because I love you in a thousand
and more.
I love you more than the ways
that exist to say hello
and I will show you love in more moments
than there are
stars in the sky.

So if you realise you have 1000
love languages that's okay.

Because learning to love you
is mine.

www.vervepoetrypress.com

@VervePoetryPres

mail@vervepoetrypress.com

THE POETS

Sanah Ahsan won the Outspoken Performance Poetry Prize 2019. Recently, she had poems shortlisted for the White Review Poet's Prize 2022; Bridport Prize 2021; National Poetry Competition 2021 and the Frontier Poetry Prize 2021. Sanah is part of the BBC Words First Alumni. Her poetry has been broadcast on Channel 4, on BBC 4's 'The Way Out' alongside Caleb Femi, and features in her TEDxLondon talk 'Rewriting my story with poetry and love as a Queer Muslim.' The Guardian described Sanah's poetry as "an exhilarating declaration of love." Sanah is currently writing her debut poetry collection with support from Arts Council England, and poets Rachel Long and Mary Jean Chan. Sanah has performed her poems across the UK, including at Shakespeare's Globe, Tate Modern, Royal Academy and Edinburgh Fringe. She has poems published in several anthologies, including Nikita Gill's 'SLAM' by Pan Macmillan. Sanah is a guest tutor for Arvon and facilitates therapeutic poetry workshops; most recently for QTBIPOC folks with a faith/spiritual background. This sold-out online space had worldwide attendees from India, Pakistan, Netherlands, US and UK. Sanah was recently the poet and lyricist for the critically acclaimed, queer theatre adaptation of The Jungle Book at The Watermill Theatre.

Garfield F. Dsouza is a freelance writer/editor/teacher/podcaster. In a career spanning over 20 years, he has copyedited Digit, a technology magazine; designed blended elearning courses for Tata Interactive Systems, Tata Power, Capgemini, Lionbridge, and Emeritus Institute of Management; and written technical documentation for IBM and Rolta. He has also conducted business -writing and analytical-thinking sessions at Larsen and Toubro and has taught the verbal section of the GMAT and SAT. He holds a bachelor's degree in Computer Engineering from the University of Mumbai and the CertTESOL from Trinity College London. 'I've been writing poetry off and on these days. And I am very hesitant to share it with the world. The little I do takes days to get my permission to be out there. Probably that's because with the poem gets uploaded a raw naked part of my self. No matter how badly or well dressed the poem may be, they reveal; and that reveal is something that frightens and thrills me.'

Ifẹ Grillo is a writer, producer, performer, and educator based in Bristol. Ifẹ's work focuses on unpacking what it means to be human in an innovative and engaging way. As a poet, Ifẹ is a Hammer and Tongue National Finalist, a Roundhouse Youth Slam National Finalist, and won the UK University National Poetry Championships in 2020. Their one-man poetry show, Ode to Heroes, was part of the UK Young Artist Festival in 2019. Ifẹ has written and created audio, written, and video content for companies including BBC Arts, Watershed, SHADO Magazine, and BBC Ideas. Last year, they were Rife Magazine's and Watershed's Creator in Residence and were one of the Co-Authors of Penguin's Black Joy Anthology. Ifẹ is now a resident artist at the Pervasive Media Studio developing their new show exploring gossip. Their background as a campaigner and advocate informs all of their practice and their work campaigning for young people led to them being appointed a trustee of the NSPCC. Ifẹ was also included in Rife Magazine's 30 Under 30 List.

Megha Harish is a queer writer of poetry and prose from Bangalore, India who works in the not-for-profit sector and enjoys walking, cooking, diving, and word games. They have been on the Barbican Young Poets programme, and performed poetry in spaces including the Tate Modern Gallery, Southbank Centre, and Fitzwilliam Museum. Their work has been published on a range of platforms in India and the UK, including Notes (Cambridge), Queerabad's Tilt, the mush newsletter, Gaysi, and The Life of Science.

Anil Pradhan (he/him) was born in a small cantonment-village called Salua, in West Bengal, India, to Indian Nepali parents who had left for and made new homes in other places. Impacted by this aspect of having multiple homes, and by virtue of his queerness, both his poetry and his research mainly focus on the intersectional politics of sexuality, migration, and memory. His ongoing doctoral research at the Department of English, Jadavpur University, Kolkata, India, focuses on the intersectional politics of sexuality, home, traversal, and memory in the context of contemporary Indian queer diasporic and immigrant literatures and cultures. Complementarily, though his poems, he has been able to share how finding home and coming to terms with and celebrating one's queerness can often be synonymous, especially for multiply marginalised folx. This intimate context has been reflected in his first book of poems titled *flitting oddments* (2020), published by Writers Workshop, Kolkata. His poems have also been published in *Café Dissensus* and *Visual Verse: An Anthology of Art and Words*. He currently resides in Kolkata.

Amani Saeed is a writer who treads the line between roots and routes. She writes poetry, blog posts, films, and whatever else is needed to get the point across. In addition to being a former member of the Roundhouse Collective, and Barbican Young Poets, Amani is the curator and host of of the interdisciplinary sell-out night the hen-nah party, designed by and for queer South Asians. Her poetry collection, *Split*, was published with Burning Eye Books. Amani is the co-writer for Queer Parivaar, which premiered at the BFI Flare 2022.

THE ORGANISERS

VERVE Poetry Festival isn't your typical literary festival. Still only four years old, it has already made a huge mark on the national poetry scene, noted for its:
    Roof-shaking spoken word sets
    Readings and workshops by award-winning poets
    Boundary-pushing poetry/theatre performances
    Lively children's events
    and much, much more!
Most importantly, Verve is a festival for everyone to enjoy
poetry together - where performance poets and page poets mingle and appreciate each others' art, where experimental poets swap numbers with childrens poets. Verve is for beginners and seasoned poetry afficiandos and everything in between. What ever kind of poet or poetry fan you are, no-one gets left out at VERVE!

The Queer Muslim Project is South Asia's largest virtual network of Queer, Muslim and allied individuals, with a growing global community of over 26K people. They use digital advocacy, storytelling and visual arts to create avenues for young people from underserved communities to express themselves, build community and forge creative collaborations.

Language is a Queer Thing is a project developed and organised by VERVE Poetry Festival and The Queer Muslim Project, funded by **The British Council, India** as part of its #India UK Together season of culture.

BBC Contains Strong Language is the UK's biggest poetry and performance festival of new writing, and is the BBC's flagship poetry and spoken word festival. Now in its sixth year, the four day festival is taking place this year in Birmingham as it welcomes the Commonwealth Games, and will broadcast live across BBC Radio and online. It was created by the BBC for Hull City of Culture in 2017, and has taken place annually since then, touring to Cumbria in 2020, Coventry in 2021, before arriving in Birmingham for 2022.

BBC Contains Strong Language 2022 is a partnership between the BBC and VERVE Poetry Festival, and is supported by Arts Council England, the British Council, The Commonwealth Games Committee and PoliNations.

ABOUT VERVE POETRY PRESS

Verve Poetry Press is a quite new and already award-winning press that focussed initially on meeting a local need in Birmingham - a need for the vibrant poetry scene here in Brum to find a way to present itself to the poetry world via publication. Co-founded by Stuart Bartholomew and Amerah Saleh, it now publishes poets from all corners of the UK and beyond - poets that speak to the city's varied and energetic qualities and will contribute to its many poetic stories.

Added to this is a colourful pamphlet series, many featuring poets who have performed at our sister festival - and a poetry show series which captures the magic of longer poetry performance pieces by festival alumni such as Polarbear, Matt Abbott and Genevieve Carver.

The press has been voted Most Innovative Publisher at the Saboteur Awards, and has won the Publisher's Award for Poetry Pamphlets at the Michael Marks Awards.

Like the festival, we strive to think about poetry in inclusive ways and embrace the multiplicity of approaches towards this glorious art.

https://vervepoetrypress.com
@VervePoetryPres
mail@vervepoetrypress.com